On the
Shoulders of Lions

On the Shoulders of Lions

Poems by

Tina Cathleen MacNaughton

THE CHOIR PRESS

First published in the United Kingdom in 2021 by
The Choir Press

ISBN 978-1-78963-197-5

Dedicated to my Dad

You did not always make it easy,
but I loved you anyway.

With thanks to my eldest son, Michael for
front cover illustration and design.

About the author

Tina lives with her husband, Andrew and divides her time between Crowthorne, Berkshire and her home city, Portsmouth. She has three sons and two grandsons. Tina is an acupuncturist, a writer and a poet and has a professional writing services company, *WriteRhymes*, which produces bespoke celebration poetry on commission.

"I am passionate about poetry. Just love it! I find reading poetry comforting, reassuring and inspirational. Writing poetry is therapeutic, liberating and insightful."

Tina may be contacted at write.rhymes@outlook.com
                          writerhymespoetry.com

Contents

On being
a woman

∽⌇∽

1

Shades of woman

As a woman I do not feel
limited
to narrow constraints
of being
sufficiently *female*
or restrained by
notions of femininity
in the same way
a boy is brought up
to be *manly.*
>A girl
>can be girly
>tomboyish
>play with dolls
>or a garage
>dress up as a fairy
>or a cowboy
>and it's generally ok.
>>She can wear flats
>>or heels
>>staid or sparkle
>>skirts long or short
>>boyfriend jeans
>>or a tux
>>bra or bra-less
>>biker boots
>>or stilettos
>>docs with florals
>>mix it up a bit
>>red lippy today
>>bare faced tomorrow

hair short, long
or in between
trousers one day
swishy dress the next.

And the good thing is
no one
bats an eye.
So there.

I wish I could swish

I wish
I had
a ponytail
to swish.

A high swishy ponytail
fresh and girly and fun
it is nubile
always fashion
has attitude
you can cock-a-hoop
with a swishy ponytail
it reinforces
a nose in the air
it's classless
equally at home
on posh
and not so posh girls*

mine is curly, thick
immobile, static, still
I do so wish
that I could swish.

---

*men have ponytails too, but they tend not to be high and swishy.

Dangly earrings

I am not complete
without a pair of earrings.
I literally have hundreds
favouring long and dangly
but
equally love a chandelier
small round pearls
and
sparkly diamond studs.

I like them all but
mostly love
the jingle, jangle
of danglies
as I walk.

They touch, they tickle
my neck pleasantly
and make me smile
I like to hold
and feel and play
with an earring
as I sit
and talk and think.

Earrings lift my mood
colour pop
a dull outfit
complement and clash
with a scarf
add pizazz
to a neutral
a touch of class
wisp of bohemian
veneer of glamour
city slick
alternative edge
they dress me up
they dress me down
I do love my earrings.

My Dear Vagina

Thank you so much
For all the pleasure
And for several children
I think it compensated
For the pain and the shame
Of our journey together.
But I must say
I feel a little let down
By You
You can't just give up
On me, you know
Now that we're free
To have more fun.
OK so you're a little drier
A little thinner, a little raw
It's not all about you
You know
A little withered
A little sore
A little atrophied
My poor dear vagina
She decided to retire early.

Sleepless Princess

She tossed and turned
And creased her pretty brow
Peeked at the clock

Though only checked just now
"I must to sleep!" she cried
She moaned, she sighed.

"This bed has lumps
The mattress is too high -
What's this I feel?"

She shook her head and said
"Who placed a sodding pea
Within one's royal bed?"

Feeling fifty-four

I'm feeling fifty-four just now.
My back aches
My mood changes on the hour.
A kind word, I'm happy

A cross one, I'm sad.
Bit like a teenager really
All moody and hormonal
Strange bleeds all over the show
My own children having children.

An ageing husband
Dying parents,
Hot and restless at night
Can't sleep or sleep for England.

A glass of wine means a hot flush
Everything feels dry and hot.
It's all a bit uncomfortable really

And the tears, they can flow
And flow ... and flow.
At this rate I'll be glad
To be an old lady.

Monday's child

Monday's child was fair of face
brought up with her cousin Trace
blue eyed, fair haired
taught to be quiet
and good
to do things properly
like a nice girl should.

She got to fifteen
looked around for a while.
Thought, *if I live like this
I shall surely die.*

So she stood up
spoke out
and laughed out loud.

It wasn't easy
to be different

But she learnt to feel proud.

I want to be too much!

You say I'm too much?
Why should I dumb down
calm down, quieten down
I want to be a harpy,
harlot, witch, scarlet woman
gossip, drama queen
loud, proud, out there
I want to shout,
laugh raucously,
giggle, cry
express myself with joy,
passion, sadness and honesty
I want to get excited
create some drama
I want to be more, not less
louder, not quieter
larger, not smaller
I want to fill my space.
You think I'm too much?
Well maybe you're insufficient,
lacking, too small,
not enough.
I don't want lacklustre, withdrawn
withheld, self-contained.
I want to make a noise
create some colour
make an entrance
don't want vanilla
don't want anodyne
don't want neutral

I want *more* of me.

One shoe

Why leave at midnight?
You can mend a dress that's torn.
Why leave one shoe
For your prince to pick up
When you can kick off two
And dance until dawn?

Ageing Vagina

Slightly withered and atrophied
(Fairly) low mileage
One responsible owner (hmmm …)
Requires lots of love and attention
And careful maintenance.
And a lot of oiling.
Enquire within.

The day I got my period and Elvis died

When I was twelve and three quarters
I was lying in bed
In my Nan's spare room
Thinking about starting
Secondary school
And noticing
My tummy hurt
Not pain exactly
More a dull ache
An unknown sensation
My Nan burst in
With a cup of tea
And lobbed *The Daily Mirror*
Straight at me.
"The King is Dead"
She pronounced
With a flourish
I thought.
I saw some brown.
I told my Nan
Who phoned my Mum
My Mum turned up
Armed with huge bulky pads
I could not bear to wear
"They're free," she said
"Knocked off from Fred."
He'd got a job lot
In his shed.
I felt sad, my tummy hurt,
I cried
August 16th
The day that Elvis died.

That time

I am a woman at that time of life
Of high-rise anxiety, wild emotions and strife
My Nan used to call it rather solemnly *"The Change"*
She seemed very hot and a little ashamed.

Up one minute, then down, then up again the next
Feeling easily riled, prone to outbursts and vexed
I used to remember and feel quite stable
Plus oodles more confident, smart and more able!

I veer very quickly from cold and then hot
And suddenly break out in an eruption of spots
It's all quite destabilising and rather disconcerting
Plus my joints are all aching, my boobs sore and hurting!

I wake after yet another long sleepless sleep
Feeling that I could lie here and silently weep
Shall I get up or remain here sadly in bed?
But this could last fifteen years, or so my Nan said!

So I get up and go and have yet another pee
(Really should not have drunk that second cuppa tea…)
Lively and irritable, not me, that's my bladder
It's weak, leaky and active and making me madder!

The hair growth, well, it's becoming a tedious chore
Plucking, waxing, exfoliation, it's all such a bore
I seriously considered growing a cute little beard
"Please don't," said my husband. "That would be *too* weird."

Once my eyes went all red and developed small styes
I rubbed, made them worse, which did not seem wise.
So I called up *Specsavers* and asked for a slot
Same day cancellation, I was there in a shot.

The eye guy looked closely with a great deal of care
I tried not to blink, but held tightly my stare
"You're now menopausal and eyes dry out with age,
It's a common story," he said, "with no cure, I'm afraid."

"Yes, I'm dry, withered and old, very prone to rage
Quite bored with this story – can we please turn the page?"
He laughed, I signed forms, said thank you and went
Oil drops were expensive, but proved money well spent!

Oh, I do love a simple and practical solution
Although it's one more task for my twice daily ablutions.
Buy hey, I see an end in view, it's somewhere in sight
Plus, I've never been one to give in and not fight.

Kind of looking forward to feeling cool, serene and quite wise
And preferably not increasing by *another* dress size.

Limitations of being a man
(particularly a straight man)

Boys don't cry
Be a Man
Man up
Sac up
Grow a pair
He lacks balls
Don't be a wimp
You're puny
Not muscular
Don't be soft
From a young age
A boy is told
To be a Man
To find the A
In Alpha Male
The capital H
In He
And most of all
The very worst
Don't be a girl
Or at all *girlie.*

The things I would do
for other men
if I was a bloke

The things I would do
for other men
if I was a bloke
and in a position of high power.

1. I would ban suits and ties
   on hot summer days
2. Give footcare and
   pedicure guidelines
   for sandal and flipflop days
3. Make wearing socks with sandals
   totally illegal
4. Pass laws to improve Christmas gifts
   for all blokes
   who generally receive
   very boring things
   socks, deodorant and hankies
   mainly.

On nature and
the elements

⚬⌒⌒⌒⚬

Afternoon walk in late summer garden

gentle summer breeze
wafts sweet breath
of blossoming flowers
soothing, calming,
caressing the senses

trailing jasmine
perfectly entwines
trellised pergola
exuding slightly exotic
subtle scent mingling with

royal lavender's
sweet, heady fragrance
tiny purple flowers
kissed by gently
humming bees

delicately danced
upon by playful
cabbage whites
waltzing from stem
to stem

towards blowsy,
overblown
white roses
fading gracefully
in shabby chic splendour

beautifully wilted as
petals, pretty still
fall softly
onto shingled pathways
in farewell.

Icy Love

Oh, the pull of the ocean
it excites, refreshes, regenerates
cools, calms, invigorates
makes me feel alive
you calm me
you call me
threaten to overwhelm me.
Cold and forbidden
an icy lover
a cold mother
freezing me out
cool and distant
yet enticing,
drawing me in.
I return again and again
to your white icicle fingers
your snowy surge
or power, energy and force
dragging me down
dragging me out,
pushing me further
further away
from what is safe
and secure.

Lying here

lying here
enshrouded
in white sheets
awakening
from dreams
warm, relaxed
sleep rich
listening
to early rain
drum against
my windowpane
the blind
lifted by a gust
like a sail
breathing in
morning freshness
lying here,
I smile
I realise
it's another day
another chance
another start
to
another day

Yellow eyed pigeon

Well, hello little pigeon

With the yellow eyes

You keep popping by

To tell me things

Yes you, little bird

You're so at home

On Mary Poppins' rooftop

Funny we should lock eyes

Just like that

You're giving me a little look

A little yellow look

Now how do I interpret that?

September

idly throw a shawl
over evening chill
as nights draw in,
golden warmth dilutes
to cooler silver sheen

as we

whisper goodbye to
last remnants
of heat and freedom,
long sun-kissed days
cherished memories

later

feelings of sorrow, loss
cast aside, forgotten,
patient autumn
gently ushers in
new, dewy freshness

whilst

sodden fungal spores
breathe out damp decay
reminiscent of death
earthy, fecund scents
suggesting promise

as

blood red berries peer
from turning leaves
transforming, preparing
for the grand finale
of fiery, valedictory colour.

Swanlets

Feeling lost, lonely
a little low,
lake beckons
calms
quietens
cools
my fire within.
Standing at water's edge
light shimmers
glimmers
sparkles
hopes, dreams
mirrored,
exposed.
Sleeping swanlets
beaks in wings
born seven
now just five.
Two died.
Swan mom
dignified,
head held high.

I too can
carry on
head high
we live
we die
we sigh.

Falling leaves, broken dreams

Walking through a woodland
Bathed in autumn glow
Scrunching through leaves,
Breathing fecund, earthy fragrance.
I glimpse tiny berries, red, white,
Sparkling like jewels
In the late autumn sunshine.

Then you capture my attention,
Your size, your beauty, your majesty
Your grace and your strength.
You shed leaves like soft, golden tears
Fluttering gently to the ground,
Letting go, just letting go.

I think you're weeping really.
Crying out lost loves, disappointments,
Past regrets, broken promises and dreams.
They all come silently, slowly down
Until you're naked, boughs undressed,
Stripped, sparse, empty, bare.

Seeming vulnerable, yet standing strong,
Resilient and quietly dignified,
Standing alone, yet deeply rooted,
As you wait quietly for winter's end,
Knowing the lighter, warmer days will come.
Understanding that you had to lose and let go
To grow stronger and more beautiful.

Midnight bugs

"Lots of bugs out there tonight
Shut the windows –
Keep the little buggers out."
"Tee hee," they laughed
A flash of shimmering silver
Weaving a little night magic
Into tomorrow's coincidences.

Sitting quietly

(First Lockdown 2020)

Sitting quietly
In my garden
Listening to leaves rustle
(I love that sound)
Feeling the sun's warmth
Touch my skin.
The birds are singing
(Do they sound happier?)
The flowers are blossoming,
A slight breeze gently wafts
Slight, subtle fragrance.
Whilst we are all inside
Mother Nature is busy,
Recreating, regenerating
And I think She is smiling.

Shadow shifting

I see a murmuration
Of starlings
Tiny flecks
Shadow dancing
Shape shifting
Swirling
Twirling
Coming together
Meeting
To make
A heart

  Transforming
  Metamorphosing
  Coming apart
  To break
  My heart

I wipe away
The tears.

BLACK BUG

window-pane corner
glimpse of black-haired legs
flash of memory,
a reminder.
You're still there then.
Thanks for the warning.

Sky watching

Sky watching last night
Dark, midnight blue
Saw Venus clear and bright
Beaming with love.
A glistening shard of light
Perhaps a shooting star?
And I thought of you
No longer here.
But when you were
You shone so bright
Had so much heart
And were so loved.

Written in memory of three of my favourite nonagenarians, Joyce, Christine and Odette. Three smart, inspirational, funny ladies – it was a pleasure to have known you.

Yearn

I hear your voice
In the rustle of leaves
Feel your warmth
In the snug of my dreams
Floating clouds
Seem to whisper
Your name
I taste your tears
In droplets of rain.

I hear you shout
As the waves
Crash the shore
Resist your pull
As you reach out
For more.

I sense you yearn
From the depths of the sea
And wonder why
You are still calling me?

On love, broken hearts and relationships

30/70

We're the same
you and I
equals in love
feels just right,
you say.
The other side
of the coin
we're meant to be
this way, forever
you say.

Words, gestures
touch and move me
opening my heart
petals unfurl, gently
one by one
to let you in.

Then when my heart
is full to melting
you give a little less
and less
I love you more
you want less
and less
on questioning, pull back
offended, hostile
I, uncomprehending
and confused
give back yet more
clumsy, desperate attempts

to redress, rebalance
address the shift.

He gives forty
I give sixty
He gives thirty
I give seventy
the more I give
the less he needs

I cry
he turns away
petals wilt, wither, die
teardrops run dry
I ask once more
He's cold, withdrawn.

Eventually I realise
with more relief than pain
I'm so tired, so very tired,
of losing this no-win game.

The Ballad of Kev and Sue

Oh, I'm so in love with you,
                    Kev said
I wish we could be wed
The thing is, I have a wife
Boring, frumpy,
          but she's my life.

She does all my washing
And always cooks my tea
She's there when I feel needy
And makes a blinding cup of tea.

But she doesn't kiss like you, Sue
And she never gives me head
So, I'd like to have you both
Please Sue, I need you in my bed!

Just don't ask me to leave her
I'm not sure how she'd cope
And I can't see you on Mondays -
It's the night we watch the soaps.

Is this all?

You had me there
In your palm
Hanging
On a thread
Waiting on your space
Your mood, your call
You very nearly
Broke me
With your coldness
With your wall
    Until one night
    I dreamt
    Of freedom
    And I wondered
    Is this all?

Tarot Reader

I went to see a tarot reader
Just needed some advice
Her eyes were sharp, her hair steel grey
She was quirky and rather nice.

I said I've found my soulmate
But feared I'd lose him too
She said he's yours for taking
And you know what to do.

So I cooked him a nice meal
Which he said was very good
He said that I looked pretty
(As he quite rightly should).

We arranged a date for dinner
On a quiet night in mid-week
I made an effort to look good
And he looked rather sleek.

We had a lovely evening
Until he said he felt quite ill
He darted to the toilet
An hour later I paid the bill.

Heartbreak Café

Sitting, stirring a cappuccino
Pretending to read a newspaper
Smiles all around, laughter
They know one another;
friends maybe
Sitting, stirring, sipping
Wishing I could be elsewhere
Anywhere but here,
Here in my head

A raucous laugh;
a snorting guffaw
The local nutter.
He likes it here too

It reminds him he could be elsewhere.

Burger Flippin' Joe

'Ello sweet 'eart
Do you want sauce on that?
Or maybe an extra scoop of fries?
He asks with a smile and a wink
Naughty, flirty Joe.
He knows how to tempt you
With an extra portion
And a nice whipped cone
With his special strawberry jus
A good helping of nuts
And a flake
On top.
It's all a bit enticing really
No, I mustn't
Oh, go on then
Joe knows how to please the ladies
He can flip my burger any day.

Crumbs ...

Why settle
For crumbs
If you can't
Have it all
A taste
Makes you
Ravenous
For more
An old tale of woe
Reels you in
Gives you hope
He belongs to her
Find your own
Sodding bloke.

Narcissist

Mirror mirror
I'm not cruel
just very selfish
as a rule
nothing personal
can't you see
it's never about you
'cos it's always, always, always
always,
always,
all about *me*.

all about *me*.
always,
always,
'cos it's always, always, always
it's never about you
can't you see
nothing personal
as a rule
just very selfish
I'm not cruel
Mirror mirror

Before

I would say your name out loud
Just so I could hear it.
I would wake
And think of You
I would think of You
First and Last
And in Between.
I'd smile at your Absence
Yearn for your Presence
Hope for your call
If we quarrelled
A deep hole.

But then I found
I could fill the gap.

First Date

Never forget when I first met her, the very stylish Sue
Fantastic girl, lovely face, her eyes were sky blue

He chatted me up, but I preferred his mate
He was still in work clothes and looked a bit of a state

I was so pleased she said yes and loved our first date
My kind of lady and really first rate!

I got there early, he was almost half an hour late
We ended up in the chippy, real classy first date!

I fancied her like mad, she was funny and down to earth
Knew I was punching quite high and well above my worth

I waited so long, was freezing cold down to my bones
I found his voice quite annoying, a deep drawl and a drone

I told her she was sexy and ever so pretty
Only problem was I didn't have that much cash in the kitty

He said he was skint, I said hey, don't be daft
I'm a feminist and insist on paying my half

I leant in quite early to get a first kiss
I puckered my lips and tried hard not to miss

He tried to come in close and nearly knocked me over
He seemed a bit drunk, I made sure I stayed sober!

She clearly liked me too and definitely fell for my charms
She clung to me as I held her tight in my arms

He talked a lot about work, I heard all his moans and groans
Plus he wouldn't stop checking his stupid bloody phone!

She's tall as a supermodel, works out and there's nothing to sag
She even let me put my fags and phone in her bag!

I suggested I look after his cigs and his phone
It was the only way to get him to leave them alone!

She's so into me, I'm a lucky guy, it's win win
She loves me, looks out for me, I'm definitely in!

He asked for my number, said he'd give me a call
Sadly I think that he's in for a fall

She's all I ever wanted and really quite chic
I'll call her after work before the football next week

He's boring, scruffy, smells of ashes and is just not my type
I gave him a made up number and a hurried goodnight!

I keep trying to call her, she must just be really busy
She still has my fags – I found her bossy and prissy!

Lonely

Whenever I feel lonely
and miss you
after just a few moments
of talking with you
I remember how lonely I felt
when I was
in a relationship
with you
and don't feel so sad.

Lazy Lover

I hate a lazy lover
You know, the type who can't be arsed
He tries to get it over with –
He wants you quick and fast

Hey, how about some foreplay?
Well, I said that you looked nice …
Perhaps a spot of post-coital?
You mean, I have to do it twice?

Could you just … you know, a little over there?
To be honest, I'm not sure … round about exactly where?
How about something special, something just for *me* …?
I thought I said the football's on – it's very nearly three?

How about a little flirt, a tiny bit of tease …?
Just a little bit of me time, don't think I'm hard to please?
Mmmm, now you're getting needy, you used to be a laugh
Instead of post-sex cuddles, why not just run yourself a bath?

Ohhh … I'd love a long lingering, sexy smouldering kiss
Take me, take me into ecstasy and sensual bliss!
Darlin', I really can't be bothered, I find soppy stuff a drag
As soon as it's all over, just need a cuppa and a fag.

Pedestal

Once I knew a guy
Said I was his Queen
Put me on a pedestal
To be admired and seen.

Did not want to touch me
Oh no, nothing so obscene
Made me feel so special
Then gradually seemed less keen

Early on he loved me madly
He said I was his world!
Then when I loved him back
Out of my life he twirled.

True

we'll sit up all night
share each other's stories
you'll tell me yours
I'll tell you mine
we'll talk through memories
past hurts, comforts, cares
beginnings and endings
we'll feel close as we share

we'll mull over details
pick apart every line
and then when it's over
we'll think back to that time
tiny inconsistencies
will worry and fret

that's when we'll realise
though our stories were true
there's always a subtext
between Me and You.

It's all love

A thoughtful, pretty card arriving out of the blue
A smile, kiss, an embrace that says I love you too
Your son places their child gently on your knee
Feeling this is right, it's where you're meant to be.

Pub lunch with a friend, sitting quietly in the snug
Laugh until you cry, say goodbye with a hug
A nod, a wave hello from a friendly passer-by
Gazing out to sea, framed by never-ending sky.

Hearing the word sorry, though you were in the wrong
Hearing love and longing in the lyric of a song.

On places

Rocksby's

Rocksby's
I miss you.
Miss your wipe-clean
plastic floral table covers
plastic lavender
in plastic pots
especially miss
your full English,
eggs fried, not poached,
just six-ninety-five
with toast, tea,
coffee or even a cappuccino
thrown in.
Miss your old-time music
just like visiting my Nan and
drinking milky coffee
on a Sunday morning.
Now you're all swished up
taken over, made over
new name, new look
my favourite
old fashioned
seaside café
all poshed up
full of loud people

with designer sunglasses
jewelled encrusted mobile phones
and other bling.
I think
I would rather sit
and drink
milky coffee
in my Nan's kitchen
any day.
Rocksby's
I loved you.
Rest In Peace.

Smokey Sydney

White sails fade
Against a cloudy sky
Like a city of ghosts,
Hushed, enshrouded
Big smoky kisses
That grasp the throat
And crinkle noses.
The taste of drought
Of heat and fire
And dust and of neglect.

We told you,
We told you so
Whispered the warm winds
We warned you
We did, we warned you
Sighed the Earth's core
We begged you
Oh we begged you
Wept the Ocean's heart.

Burn baby burn
Flames dance and die
And dance again.
Ashes scatter
Dust settles
Embers crackle.

Portsmouth

You shine.
Never apologising for being
next to Southampton
Plymouth has hills
you're flat
and don't strain backs
crowded terraced streets
with no parking
embracing huge expanse
of Southsea Common
and the sea.

Gettcha-five-a-day
in-a-brown-paper-bag
at the Fair
or a colonic busting burger.
Portsmouth's got it all.
Posh cocktails by the Wharf
living it up like a millionaire
or 2-for-1 at Spoons.
Portsmouth,
you encompass everything
and everyone.

And I love you for it.
Portsmouth,
You are beautiful.

Swindon

You are boring.
The party that never got going
The dress that failed to impress
The meal that lacked spice
The coffee that didn't deliver
The apology that lacked feeling
The excuse that didn't hold up
The lie that didn't ring true

Out-edged by Bristol
Out-shone by Oxford

Swindon.
You are boring.

On memory
and death

I wrote this poem after reading an article in a magazine in the back of a taxi to Warsaw airport. It was a personal testimony by a survivor of The Warsaw Uprising and the story stayed with me. Obviously also inspired by one of my old favourites, Philip Larkin's monumental poem, *An Arundel Tomb*. My poem is a tribute to bravery and kindness.

I think he got it wrong

I've thought about this hard and long
and I think the poet
got it wrong
what will persist
is kindness, only kindness.

Small boy, sixteen
standing there
shaking, scared
trying to be strong
in a black world where
evil and terror ruled

A pull on his arm
a whisper,
"Come, you are my son"
another mother, a new one
trembling, afraid, but sure
this is what must be done.

And he was saved
from digging his own grave
for daring to resist
saved to fight, to live
saved by a brave heart
jolted into action.

I've thought about this hard and long
and yes, I'm afraid
he did get it wrong
what will persist
is kindness,
only kindness.

In memory of those who were not so fortunate,
The Warsaw Uprising, 1st August 1944 – 2nd October 1944.

Just seventeen

Sidney Rex **STOP** just another name **STOP** amongst thousands
STOP set in cold black stone **STOP** Southsea Common Memorial,
Portsmouth **STOP** signed up just seventeen **STOP**
stepped aboard proudly **STOP** *Glow Worm* **STOP** "first class stoker,
sir" **STOP** torpedoed **STOP** by German submarine **STOP** missing in
action **STOP** Sidney Rex **STOP** presumed dead **STOP**

never a trace
of Sidney Rex
heartbroken mother
died
eighteen months later
leaving eight more sons
and a daughter,
Violet Doris,
my nan
just seventeen also
STOP

Stone

Small hand tightly clasped in yours
race to the top of steep stone steps
I squeal and laugh, you lift me high
onto the shoulders of lions
a little war torn, chipped,
but stone cold solid.

To the Queen's park,
feed the birds, peacocks fanning
posturing, preening
leapfrog over lily pads
through hot, steamy greenhouse
full of colour, exotica
another world, another stone,
gravestone.

Kiss the photo
of the pretty, dark-eyed lady
she's been waiting for you, patiently
she's been sleeping
for quite some while.
You miss her still.

Stroke the little canary
pet set in stone,
hard, ice-cold marble,
but fragile still,
a little lost, bereft,
reminding us of what was
what could have been
what is missed.

And now you rest alongside
the dark-eyed lady
in peace, eternity, in unison
in sadness and in joy
in love, death, in memories,
set in stone.

In memory of Elvis

Elvis, you got us all shook up
in your leathers and blue suede shoes
you broke our wooden hearts
you big hunk of love!
Couldn't help falling in love with you
loved you tender
were burnt up with love
just one night with you
would be too much
even for a hard-headed woman.
So don't be cruel
'cos now and then there's a fool such as I
you may have gone
but you are always on our minds
that was the wonder … ('da da da da')
the Wonder of You!

Hawk

voicemail message
changes everything
first few words heard
the rest made up
I wail,
deep, guttural, animal cry

moment of numbness
followed by
flurry of activity
lost in own bedroom
pacing, confused.
Uncomprehending.

Somehow manage everyday routines
washing, cleaning teeth, dressing

the drive down
passenger seat, bent,
head in hands, weeping
songs on radio
pick at memories.
I weep some more.

Spy a hawk
perched low
on tree roadside
watching, guiding
marking the journey
to childhood home.

More weeping, wailing
carpet picnic, curtains drawn
undrawn.
Bright sunlight blindly
inappropriate,
darkness worse.

You hated to be closed in,
contained.
We swap stories, reminisce
lots of cups of tea
lot of laughing,
surprisingly.

Yesterday you were pale,
but breathing
and there
in that chair
now empty.
An absence of you.

Drive home
guided by Capricorn supermoon
big, white, ominous
first day of the year
and you are gone.
I think of the hawk.

You loved birds.

Amy, we loved you

Loved you Amy
loved your talent
feisty, yet fragile
those raw, old soul lady notes
cracked with love and longing
bare with the pain and shame
of loving too much
we listened to your voice
always poised at the edge
of heartbreak,
we watched your pretty, plump self
dwindle and disappear
some laughed as you fell down,
drunken and disorientated,
stumbling for words on stage
others saw a troubled girl
emotions too deep, too open
whittled down to nothing
as addictions grew
and took over
obsession for your guy
and other substances
stole the life from you,
such sadness in those eyes
peering out
from big, black nest hair
searching, curious, lost
shabby ballet pumps
on spindly little legs
just a girl really

who sung her heart out,
loved and gave too much
who had it all
and lost it
we watched you squander
that rare, honest talent
as you became a wisp of yourself
before our eyes
and we lost you too, Amy
God bless you,
not always understood
but loved by so many.

Never goodbye

Feel your breath
As the wind wafts the trees
Feel you're here
In a vast, empty space
Hear you whisper
In a silent, stone-walled church
Hear your voice
In the quiet hum of bees
Feel your kiss
On a warm summer's breeze
Sense your smile
In the sunshine's rays.
Hello You
Yes.
It's been quite a while.

Final word on relationships

I sometimes feel that love, friendship, all our relationships, however big, small, easy, difficult, simple or complicated are all significant and never really leave us. Whether we have lost someone through death, dwindling love, shift in feelings, geographical distance or sheer disappointment they are always with us, etched in our heart, one way or another. So, it's never really goodbye. We hold onto a little piece of each other whether we want to or not.

A little bit of whimsy

Silvergrey

I like to think
my life is not Golden
but mainly Silver
sprinkled with
occasional stardust
and gold and gems
that sparkle,
excite and
lift me
above the swathes
of Greyness
that sometimes
threaten to suffocate
and drown
my soul
until they pass,
as they always do.
I know I need
both Golden
and Greyness
to appreciate
the mainly
Silver times.

Small pleasures

Resting quietly, warm cat snuggled sleepy on knee
Pleasant, calm thoughts, hot strong cup of tea

Subtle scent of jasmine, growing freely, fragrant, wild
Holding onto hand of beloved, precious child

Feeling clean, refreshed after long hot soapy shower
Admiring moon and stars, distant beauty, celestial power

Cocooning gurgling baby in fluffy towel after bath
Sharing food and wine, good friends, we talk, we laugh

Tasting rich dark chocolate slowly melting on my tongue
Cycling through woods, free, alive, girlish, young

Quiet hush of leaves rustling gently on cool light breeze
Dancing to music, singing, flirting, being teased.

Waking to morning raindrops, in bed warm and snug
Feeling held, safe, accepted, embraced in loving hug.

Inspired by my grandsons, Edward and Sebastian. Grandchildren put love and happiness back into perspective – keep it simple.

Free

Staying away is now love
Though it may seem unfair
Distance is kindness
And kindness is care.

This time will soon pass
We're going to be alright
Sometimes sitting quietly
Is the best way to fight.

Each day that we do this
Is a day towards being free
When your world is less busy
You learn to accept and just be.

And when you know how to *be*
Well, then you really are free.

Legacy of 2020 pandemic – having to learn to keep away from one another.

Scorpio Moon

She stood under the lamp-post
she looked up at the moon
thought of friends and lovers
those lost
    and some too soon.

she cast a smoky eye
down onto damp, dark ground
black thoughts of past desires,
birth, death
    it all comes round.

she pursed her scarlet lips
and reached out for her phone
she checked, shook her head
and gave
    a gentle groan

her heels clicked as she walked
glanced at the midnight sky
mystery, desire, secrets, lies
she walked away
    her head held high.

Sunday

It's Sunday
The sun is shining
I don't have any plans
But I'm happy, happy, happy.

The sky is blue
I open the kitchen window
The cold, fresh air wafts in
It's nice outside.

Might go for a walk
Or have a cup of tea
The house is warm
It's Sunday and I'm happy,
Happy just being me.

The Spell of the Gypsy Queen

By the mystical light of the midnight moon
The Gypsy Queen quietly constructs her rune

Singing so softly, a strange haunting tune
Working swiftly, knowing her spell must end soon

Mingling snowflakes, rose petals, pungent herbs
Stirring in starlight with the feather of a bird

Dancing and swaying in her long purple cloak
Sprinkling moon beams into dewdrops to soak.

She whispers in rhymes from a long time ago
Moves to a rhythm so few longer know,

Her aura is golden, her power at its height
A glance in the mirror, she swoops into the night

Full moon silhouetted, an owl ghostly white
Glides into the world to put misdeeds right.

cuppa tea

a cuppa tea for two
is such a comforting thing to do
clink of cups in saucers
little laugh over milk first or last
another joke about still needing sugar
aren't we sweet enough?
if cubes, a satisfying clunk
is heard.
shall we be naughty and have a biccy?
or go mental and have a slice of cake?

it's all a delight
but most of all
a good cuppa strong tea
almost always, always
makes you feel better
about the world.
It's just a fact.

What I've learnt

I've reached the Autumn years of life
and this is what I've learnt -
I'm glad I'm brave and grabbed at life
although I have been burnt ...

I've learnt I'm happy on my own
better with family and friends
I've learnt who's in my corner -
who's a vampire or a dead end.

I've learnt there's different kinds of love -
there are flatterers v. those I trust
I've learnt the difference between true love
and good old-fashioned lust ...

I've learnt some people can't be fathomed
and frankly I don't care
I've been knocked down,
                    but I got up ...
a fragile heart
it seems
repairs.

Pic 'n' Mix

⌘

The day I voted for Cameronen

The day I voted for the Tories
I drove home, fingers crossed
Hoped at least I'd kept out JC
Please God that Labour lost.
As a citizen I'd done my bit
Kept Britain from disaster
Although it would be no mean feat
Oh no, not happy every after.
Spotted lady flustered roadside
Shooing some invisible thing
A sudden thud and then she cried,
Held up a battered wing.
We stared in double shock
At pheasant suddenly deceased
Poorly smashed up cock
His blood and guts unleashed.
Unfortunate messy omen
The day I voted for Cameronen.

Ultra-cautious yoga teacher

And breeeeeeathe …This is your time. Just for you. For you to totally relax. Now, take a nice deep breath, just for you. Time to de-stress. Not to worry about anything. Could you just take your socks off please, my lovely? Don't want you to slip over there. Sticky bud socks? That's OK then. Now … breeeeeeathe. Just let it all go. Joyce, Joyce – could you just watch your back there please my lovely – yes, that's it. Not too far. Don't want that disc going again, do we? Just relax now ladies … that's it, don't worry about anything or anyone. Pat, Pat, do you want to put a nice rolled up blanket under your knees there for your moving cats and cows? That's it, don't want an 'op' on the other one, do we now? And Julie – yes, you my dear, don't put your head down too far. Not with your cholesterol. That's right lovey. And breeeeeeathe … let it all out. Just relax. Oooh, watch that neck of yours, Amy – just a semi-circle – don't go all full moon on me please. Don't want you getting a crick. Not again. Now ladies, open your eyes really wide with this one – unless you wear contact lenses of course. Don't want those popping out all over the show. Could cause a nasty accident. Jean, put your socks back on for this one, lovey – I can see your poorly circulated feet going blue from here. Yes, I know, but I can't see you realistically striding too wide, can you? Not with those ankles. Now breeeeeeathe … . Close your minds to any worries or concerns and don't think about anything else at all. This is your time …your space … just for you. Now Samantha …

Why I call someone a ****

It's such a satisfying word
Those hard consonants
Perfectly spat out
To illustrate true contempt
Sharp, short, effective
The power of perfectly
Enunciated
Female genitalia.
It shocks
But should never
Be overused
Is never said lightly
Nor without feeling
Nor very good reason
No, if I call you a ****
You have hurt me
Harmed my family
Cheated on me
Lied to me
Disrespected me
Deeply wounded me
Taken the piss with me
Trampled on my boundaries
Seriously offended my values.
So, when I call you a ****
You will have pulled
Some kind of stunt
And probably deserved it.

Fruity Frederick!

Oh, us village ladies do love Freddy
Always stood at his stall, good and ready

Get your five a day here and some more,
I've got wonderous goodies galore!

You know what they say, keeps the GP away
Two quid for five apples – I eat one every day!

He does like an advert, a blatant promotion
And when he starts singing, it's quite a commotion!

Environmentally friendly and good for the planet
Try my plums, they're homegrown, just a quid for a punnet!

He'll pack up your fruit in a brown paper bag
(Then sneak out the back for a quick cheeky fag).

He'll draw funny pictures on those bags made of paper,
Oh, Fred loves a joke and a laugh and a caper!

Apples, pears, bananas, all in peak, peachy condition
Try one of my cherries, you have my permission!

He'll give you a nod, a wink and a big cheeky grin
Oh, he'd get away with murder if you'd just let him!

When Fred's feeling exotic, he sells melon and figs
If he feels a bit cold, then he'll dance a quick jig.

Keep your fruit bowl attractive and full to the brim
Then you'll eat less cake and keep your hips nice and trim!

Oh Frederick, you're cheeky and we like you a lot
Do we mind if you're naughty? Oh no, we do not!

Envy

I am only

    A little envious

        Of other people

            When they expect

                So very little.

                    And seem so happy.

Sneeze

Walking along
Keeping myself
    to myself
    in a safe bubble
    step onto road
    to avoid old man
        who turned
        and sneezed
        his droplets
        all over me.
        "Sorry," he said.
        Well, that's alright then.

Poetry Therapy

If I write you into a poem
perhaps I can make you disappear

reduce you to word, shape, form
craft you into a few carefully spun ideas

turn you into nonsense
a mere rhyme
without reason.

I can make you twist and turn
and do as I command
I can imbue you with meaning
        or not

        and yet
still you rise
construed, yet not wholly
constructed,
        by my imagination

gasping a new breath
        and extending beyond
                the boundaries

I try hard to reposition.

THE END